My Best Book of

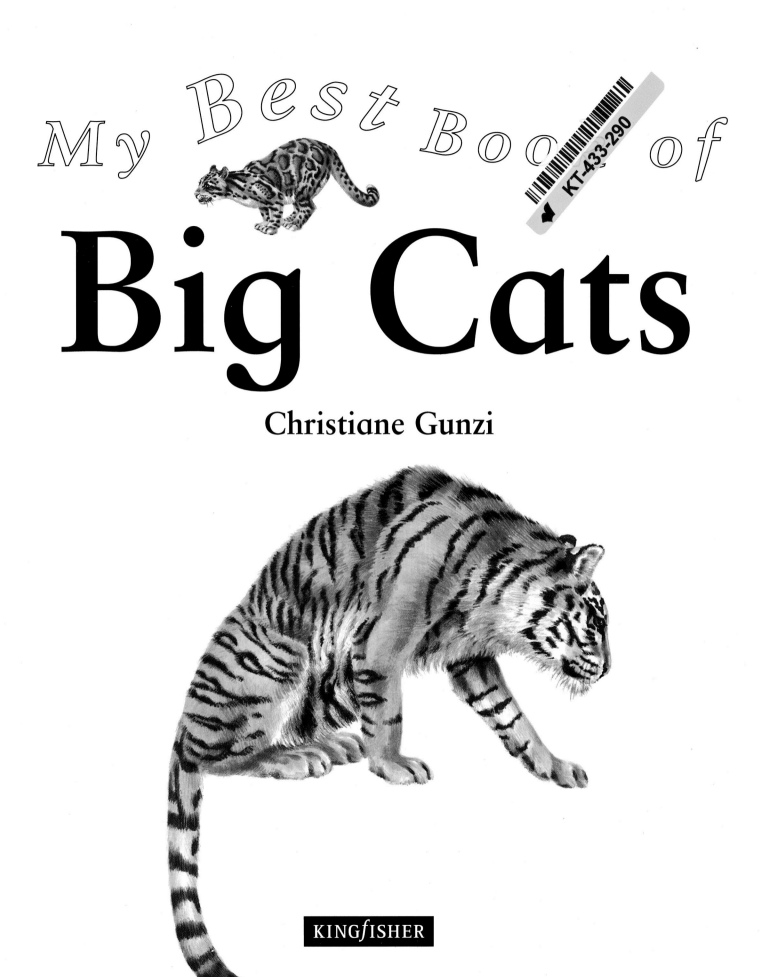

Big Cats

Christiane Gunzi

KINGFISHER

Contents

Created for Kingfisher by
Picthall & Gunzi Limited

Author and editor: Christiane Gunzi
Designer: Floyd Sayers
Editorial assistance: Lauren Robertson and
Jill Somerscales
Natural history consultant: Julie Childs
Illustrators: Martin Knowldon and Mick
Loates

KINGFISHER
Kingfisher Publications Plc,
New Penderel House,
283–288 High Holborn,
London WC1V 7HZ
www.kingfisherpub.com

First published in hardback
by Kingfisher Publications Plc 2001

First published in paperback
by Kingfisher Publications Plc 2002

10 9 8 7 6 5 4 3 2 1

1TR/0302/WKT/MAR(MAR)/128KMA

1TS/0804/WKT/MAR(MAR)/128MA/F

A CIP catalogue record for this book
is available from the British Library.

ISBN 0 7534 0542 3 (hardback)
ISBN 0 7534 0684 5 (paperback)

Printed in Hong Kong

Meet the big cat

Big cats such as tigers, lions and leopards are powerful meat-eaters or carnivores. Their strong claws and sharp teeth help them to hunt other animals to eat. Big cats have excellent hearing and sight, sleek, muscular bodies and beautiful fur coats. Today, many big cats are endangered because people kill them for their fur. The most endangered big cat is the tiger.

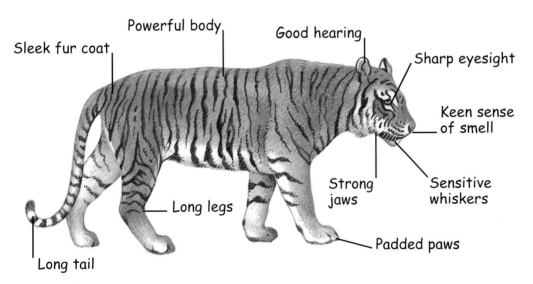

Sleek fur coat

Powerful body

Good hearing

Sharp eyesight

Keen sense of smell

Strong jaws

Sensitive whiskers

Long legs

Padded paws

Long tail

A big cat's body

The cat's muscular body and long legs allow it to leap, pounce and climb, and its long, flexible tail helps it to balance. On the underside of each foot are pads that act as cushions when the cat lands on hard ground. A big cat's large eyes can see well in the dark, and its funnel-shaped ears can turn to catch the smallest sound. Long, sensitive whiskers on its face help the cat to feel its way.

4

Siberian tiger

This is the largest, most powerful cat in the world, and only about 200 are left in the wild. The Siberian tiger's long, thick fur keeps it warm in the cold forests of China, Siberia and Korea where it lives. In winter, its coat becomes paler in colour, so pigs, deer and other prey cannot see it as easily.

A world of big cats

Big cats have lived on Earth for about 34 million years, and they all belong to the same family. They are found on every continent except Australia and Antarctica. Big cats include lions, tigers, jaguars and leopards. The cheetah is a close relative, but it is different from other cats because it has narrow paws and blunt claws, like a dog. Apart from the cheetah, jaguar and clouded leopard, all these cats can roar. The lion's roar is the loudest.

Well disguised

Big cats are famous for their magnificent coats. Cats in hot countries have shorter fur than those in cold countries. The colours and markings on a cat help it to blend in with its habitat. This disguise is called camouflage. Lions have sand-coloured coats to camouflage them in dry savannah areas, and tigers have stripes to camouflage them in forests.

Clouded leopard
(Asia)
weighs 23kg
up to 1.3m long

Jaguar
(South America)
weighs 46-113kg
1.3-1.5m long

Snow leopard
(Asia)
weighs 25-75kg
1.2-1.5m long

Lion
(Africa)
weighs 132-180kg
up to 2m long

Tiger
(Asia)
weighs 180-260kg
2.7-3m long

Cheetah
(Africa)
weighs 45-60kg
1.3-1.5m long

Leopard
(Africa and Asia)
weighs 65-80kg
1-1.3m long

7

Growing up

Young big cats are called cubs. They grow inside their mother's body for about three months, then she gives birth to them in a safe place, such as a den or a cave. The cubs are born covered with fur, but they cannot see well or walk properly for a few days. Young cats stay with their mother until they are old enough to hunt for themselves.

Baby tigers

1 A tigress has between two and four cubs in a litter. They feed on her milk for six to eight weeks. Then she will bring them prey to eat.

2 A tiger cub learns to hunt by playing. After a few months, its mother will take it on hunting trips when it will learn to catch prey.

3 At 11 months old, a tiger cub can catch birds by itself. At 16 months old, it is big enough to hunt larger prey, such as deer.

Cat courtship

Big cats that are friends often greet each other with a head rub. Male and female tigers breed once a year, usually in spring. After mating, the male leaves the female. When the cubs are born, the female cares for them on her own.

A good mother

Every few days, the female leopard carries her cubs to a new hiding-place so that jackals, hyenas and wild dogs cannot find them. Sometimes she has to leave the cubs hidden for several days while she goes in search of food.

Perfect hunters

Lions, tigers and other big cats are expert hunters. They have powerful legs for chasing, and strong jaws and sharp teeth for biting. Big cats eat all kinds of animals – gazelles, wild pigs, rabbits and fish. Usually hunting at dawn or dusk, they silently creep up on their prey. They pounce quickly, and grab the animal by the neck or throat.

Catching prey

Lions are the only big cats that hunt animals larger than themselves. Lionesses often hunt in groups. They chase antelopes, zebras, gazelles and wildebeest. Although the lionesses do the hunting, the lions always eat first.

Lionesses chasing
a young oryx

10

Pouncing tiger

Tigers usually hunt alone at night, and often close to water. Before they pounce on prey, such as muntjac deer, they have to get close to them, because tigers can only run in short bursts.

Cat talk

Big cats make all sorts of sounds to communicate with each other. They purr, growl, hiss and roar. One big cat will signal to another by twitching its tail and moving its ears. An angry cat will growl and flick its tail to warn another cat not to come into its territory. If rival cats get into a quarrel, the smaller, weaker animal usually gives in to the larger, stronger one before a fight can begin.

Roaring

A lion roars to talk to other members of his pride. This is the loudest sound made by any cat and it travels a long way.

Making faces

People can tell a lot about big cats by watching their eyes and ears. If a cat is happy and content, it sits with its eyes half-closed. If it is frightened or surprised, its eyes are big and round. Ears flat on the head mean that the cat is annoyed or afraid. When a cat is really angry, it holds its ears close to its head, opens its mouth wide and shows its long canine teeth as a warning to other animals.

Content (eyes half-closed)

Alert (ears pricked)

Frightened (eyes wide open)

Angry (ears flattened)

Who's boss?

When one cat is afraid of another cat, it lies down to show that it does not want to fight. The bigger, stronger cat flattens its ears and looks menacing to show that it is the boss.

Smilodons

These sabre-toothed cats lived in family groups in North and South America. They killed mammoths and other large mammals with their long, sharp teeth. The last *Smilodons* died out about 8,000 years ago.

The first big cats

More than 20 million years ago the first relatives of today's big cats lived on Earth. They are known as the sabre-toothed cats and they looked a bit like lions and leopards. Sabre-toothed cats were carnivores with massive canine teeth for killing and eating their prey. The sabre-toothed cat that we know most about is *Smilodon*. It was slightly larger than today's lion and very fierce.

Sabre-toothed cat

Lion

Open wide

The sabre-toothed cat could open its mouth very wide. It had such long teeth that, when it closed its mouth, they stayed on the outside.

A modern-day lion has smaller canine teeth than its ancient relatives. It does not need such large teeth because it kills prey by suffocation, and not by biting.

Lion king

Lions are the largest, most powerful cats in Africa. A few lions are also found in India.

Lions live in family groups called prides, and there can be up to 30 lions in one pride. The male lion is the only big cat with a mane around the head and chest. This thick fur makes him look larger than he really is, and helps him to frighten away enemies. The mane also protects a lion during a fight.

Family pride

The male lion does not help the female lionesses to raise cubs. His job is to protect the pride against intruders. If a rival tries to enter his territory, he roars loudly. If two lions fight, the winner becomes king of the pride. The loser has to leave and find somewhere else to live.

Scratching post

A lion scratches trees to mark his territory. He leaves claw marks and a strong smell to show others that this is his home. The next time the lion passes by, he sniffs the spot to check that his scent is still there.

Catnap

A pride of lions spends much of its time relaxing and sleeping. Lions only hunt when they are hungry and the males leave the hunting to the females. Sometimes lions eat remains of food left by hyenas and other scavengers.

Lions use their teeth and claws when they fight over territory.

Cool cat

The tiger is one of the most magnificent creatures on Earth. This powerful predator lives deep in the forest, where it stalks deer and wild pigs in the long grass. It spends much of its time hunting, and must eat about 100 large prey a year. Tigers need a huge area to hunt in, and their territory can be as large as 160 square kilometres. Apart from the jaguar, the tiger is the only big cat that enjoys water.

White tiger

Tigers with pale fur are called white tigers. They are very rare. White tigers have brown stripes instead of black stripes, and their eyes are blue instead of yellow.

Tiger types

Scientists believe that there are only about 5,000 tigers living in the wild. The five types that survive today are the Siberian, Bengal, Caspian, Sumatran and Indo-Chinese tigers. These cats are found in Asia, and are all in danger of extinction.

The Caspian tiger has the longest fur

The Siberian tiger has the palest fur

The Sumatran tiger has the closest stripes

The Bengal tiger has the shortest fur

The Indo-Chinese tiger has the darkest fur

18

Storing food

When a tiger catches a deer or other big animal, it usually drags it to a quiet place. This can sometimes be as far as 1km away. When the tiger has eaten enough, it covers the dead animal with leaves and grass so that other creatures cannot smell it. The tiger may return later to finish its meal.

Tiger lazing in a forest stream to keep cool

Leopard's lunch

Leopards eat all sorts of animals, including big and small birds, small mammals, medium-sized mammals and insects. After eating, leopards like to go and drink at a waterhole.

Cricket

Aardvark

Rabbit

Hornbill

Ostrich

Baboon

A heavy meal

A leopard's prey can weigh as much as the leopard itself. It is hard work for the cat to carry its meal up into a tree. The leopard uses the branches of a tree for storing and protecting its food to eat later.

Spotted killer

The leopard is good at climbing, and often carries its prey into the branches of trees, to keep it safe from hyenas, jackals and other scavengers. Leopards live alone for most of the time, and they can survive in all kinds of habitat, including the forests of Asia and the African savannah. A leopard's eyesight and hearing are six times better than a human's. This helps leopards escape from poachers, who want to kill them for their beautiful coats.

Leopard dragging
a dead gazelle
into a tree

Black magic

A panther is, in fact, a black leopard. If you look at its coat closely, you can just see its leopard spots. Black panthers live like other leopards. They are found in the forests of Asia and some areas in Africa, and they are becoming very rare.

Cloudy coat

The clouded leopard lives in the forests of India, Nepal and southeast Asia, and is hardly ever seen. Its teeth look more like a sabre-toothed cat's than any other cats' teeth. Unlike other leopards, this one does not roar.

21

Secretive cat

Jaguars live deep in the South American rainforests. They are good tree climbers and, unlike most other cats, are excellent swimmers and like to live near water. Jaguars usually hunt at night for mice, deer and other mammals. They also eat turtles and frogs, and catch fish. When a jaguar goes fishing it will wait on the bank and flip fish out of the water with a paw. Most jaguars have dappled coats, but some are black. A black jaguar (seen here resting in a tree) does have spots, but its markings can hardly be seen.

Spot the difference

Jaguars and leopards look quite similar, even though they live in different parts of the world. A jaguar's body and legs are more stocky than a leopard's, and its jaw is wider. A jaguar's spots are also larger than the spots on a leopard.

Leopard

Jaguar

Champion racer

The cheetah is the fastest mammal on Earth. With its slim body and long legs, it is the perfect shape for running and leaping. The cheetah lives on the African savannah. While lions and leopards are sleeping during the day, the cheetah hunts for antelopes, gazelles, hares and rodents. Male cheetahs usually live in groups of four or five, and they guard their territory fiercely. Females usually live alone, except when they are looking after a litter of cubs.

From standing still, a cheetah can reach top speed in three seconds.

Hiding in the grass

To keep newborn cheetah cubs safe from leopards, hyenas and other predators, their mother carries them to a new hiding-place every few days. The cubs usually live with their mother for up to 20 months. They have long, greyish fur on their backs. This may help to disguise them when they hide in long grass.

Fast as the wind

In short bursts, a cheetah can chase prey at speeds of up to 100km an hour – more than twice as fast as the best human runners.

Run for your life

Gazelles flee when they see a cheetah. The cheetah chases them, but if it does not catch one after a minute or so, it has to stop because it gets tired.

Cat cousins

The big cats also have many smaller relatives. The puma, lynx, serval, ocelot and caracal are all wild cats. These cats are related to the domestic cats that people have at home. Most of the smaller wild cats live in wooded areas, on high mountains or even in hot deserts. They cannot roar like the big cats, and their young are called kittens, instead of cubs. Smaller wild cats hunt rats, mice, rabbits, birds and insects, just like domestic cats.

Puma
(North and South
America)
weighs 36-103kg
96cm to 2m long

Cat acrobats

All these wild cats are quick and agile, and they climb and jump well. They usually hunt animals smaller than themselves, and can leap high into the air to catch birds and insects as they fly past.

Siberian Lynx
(Asia)
weighs 8-28kg
60cm to 1.3m long

Ocelot
(North and South
America)
weighs 11-15kg
55cm to 1m long

**African wildcat
(Africa)
weighs 3-8kg
50-75cm long**

**Caracal
(Africa and India)
weighs 6-19kg
60cm to 91cm long**

**Serval
(Africa)
weighs 9-18kg
67cm to 1m long**

Tiger in the house

Domestic cats learn how to survive by playing, just like big cats do. When you see a kitten pouncing on a ball of wool, it is quite easy to imagine its cousins hunting in the wild.

**Lynx
(North America)
weighs 5-17kg
80cm to 1m long**

27

Big cats in danger

Every year, huge areas of land are cleared to make space for houses, roads and farms. Forests, grasslands and other habitats are destroyed. These areas are home to big cats and many other animals. When animals lose their home, it is difficult for them to find food and shelter. If we do not protect the places where big cats and other wild animals live, one day they will only live in zoos and wildlife reserves.

Birds flee from their homes to escape a blazing fire.

Burning bright

When a grassland or forest is burned to clear land, the animals and plants that live there are in danger, and many are killed. These areas are the habitat of tigers, leopards and other rare mammals

Poaching

People have been hunting big cats for their fur for thousands of years. Today, it is illegal to kill wild cats, but a few people still hunt them. The animal's fur, bones, teeth and meat are sold. It is difficult to protect big cats in the wild from poachers. The cats roam over huge areas and there are not enough people to guard them.

Guards arrest a poacher in Africa.

The skins of leopards and other big cats have been made into fur coats.

Why big cats are killed

In some parts of the world, cats are killed to make fur coats, and their bones are used in medicines. This is not necessary, because coats can be made from fake fur, and ingredients other than big cat bones can be used in medicines.

Powdered tiger bones have been used in medicines, because some people believe they have special powers.

The teeth of big cats have been made into jewellery.

29

Studying big cats

It is important to protect big cats in the wild so that we can save them from extinction. Experts watch cats in their natural habitat to find the best way to look after them. They may put a collar with a radio transmitter around a cat's neck. The transmitter sends out signals that help the experts to follow the cat and discover where it likes to live in the wild.

A group of lionesses in a safari park

Tracking big cats

The snow leopard is found only in the high mountains of Asia, so it is difficult to track it down unless it has a radio collar on. Radio collars help scientists to find and take care of these beautiful cats in the wild.

Seeing big cats up close

You can see big cats at a safari park or in a wildlife reserve, where they have lots of room to roam around. Visitors can drive along and watch the cats from the safety of a car or jeep. It is not safe to get out of the car when you are with big cats.

Glossary

camouflage The different colours and markings on an animal that help it to hide in the wild.

canine teeth The long, pointed teeth that cats have, for eating meat.

carnivores Animals, such as cats, that eat meat.

carrion An animal that has been killed, but is not yet completely eaten. Animals, called scavengers, will eat the remains.

communicate This is how all animals talk to each other. It may be by smell, by voice, or by the way that the animals stand or move.

domestic cat A small cat that lives with people.

endangered An animal or plant that is in danger of dying out forever. Many big cats are endangered.

extinct An animal or plant that has died out forever. Mammoths and sabre-toothed cats are extinct.

habitat An animal's habitat is its natural home in the wild. A cheetah's natural habitat is the African savannah.

illegal There are laws to protect all of us, including big cats. Something that is against the law is illegal. It is illegal to kill big cats.

mammals Animals, such as cats, that are covered with fur or hair, give birth to live young and feed them milk.

mane This is the long, thick fur on a lion's head and shoulders. The lion is the only big cat that has a mane. It makes him look bigger than he really is.

poachers People who hunt and kill wild animals, such as big cats, are called poachers. It is against the law to poach big cats.

predators Animals that hunt and prey on other animals. Cats are predators.

prey These are animals that are hunted and eaten by cats and other predators.

pride This is the name for a family group of lions. Lions are the only big cats that live in family groups.

rodents Small mammals, such as rats, mice and squirrels, are rodents. They are prey for big cats.

savannah Huge, flat areas of grassland in Africa, with only a few trees.

scavengers These are animals that search for food left by other animals. Hyenas, jackals and vultures are scavengers.

stalk To stalk is to follow an animal quietly. Tigers stalk their prey.

territory The area where an animal lives. Big cats have large territories.

Index